William Bolcom

Concert-Piece

for B♭ Clarinet and Piano

Concert-Piece is recorded on MSR1314 by Maureen Hurd and Blair McMillen: "SPELUNK: Premieres for Clarinet"

ISBN 978-1-4234-4267-7

EDWARD B. Marks Music Company / EXCLUSIVELY DISTRIBUTED BY HAL•LEONARD® CORPORATION
7777 W. BLUEMOUND RD. P.O. BOX 13819 MILWAUKEE, WI 53213

www.ebmarks.com
www.halleonard.com

for Morton Subotnick

Concert-Piece
for Bb Clarinet and Piano

DURATION: ca. 13:00

I

WILLIAM BOLCOM
(1959)

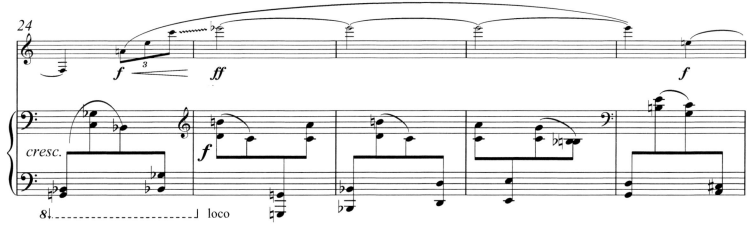

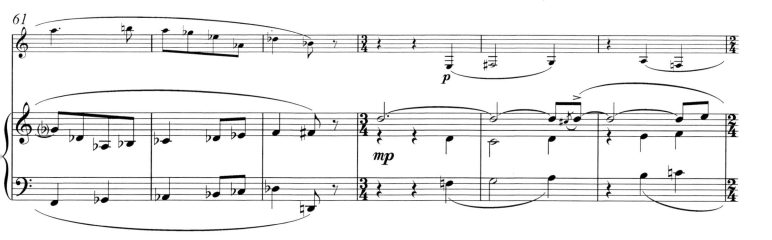

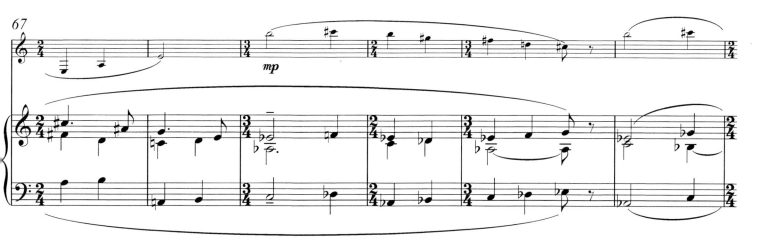

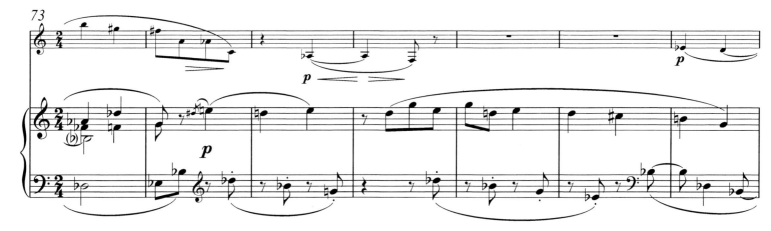

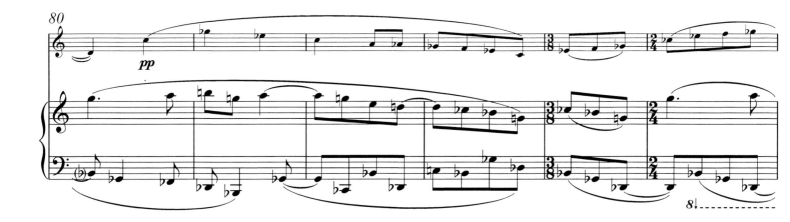

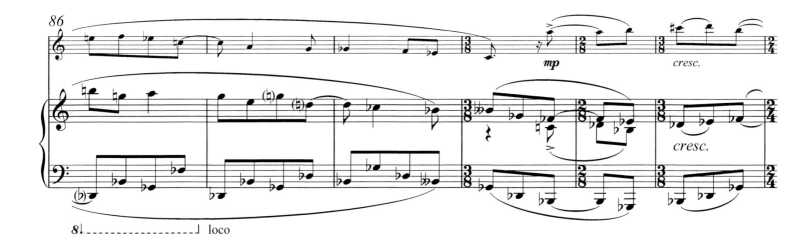

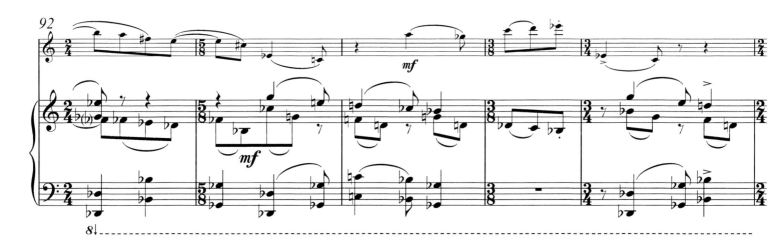

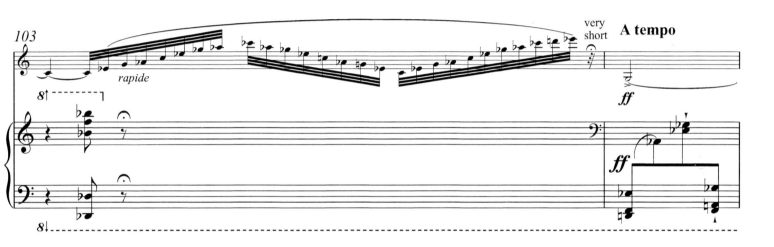

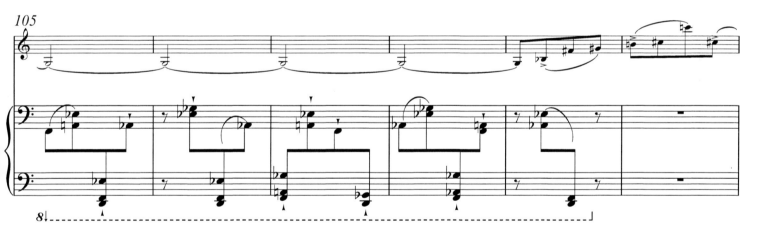

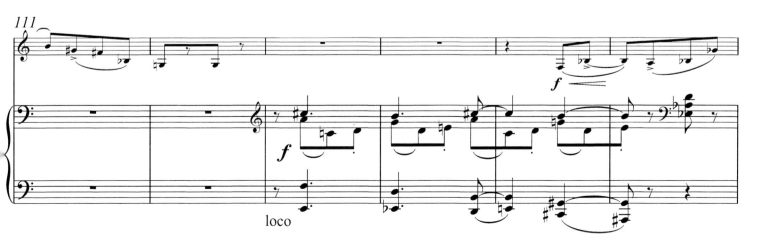

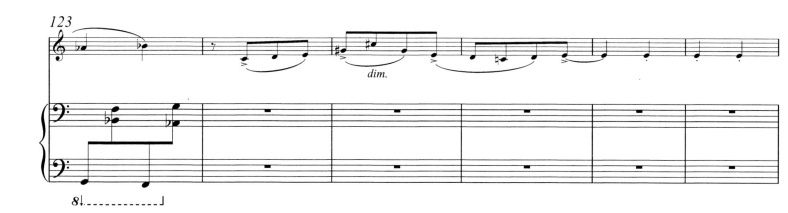

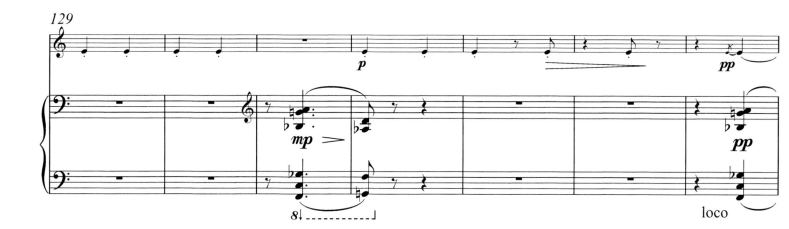

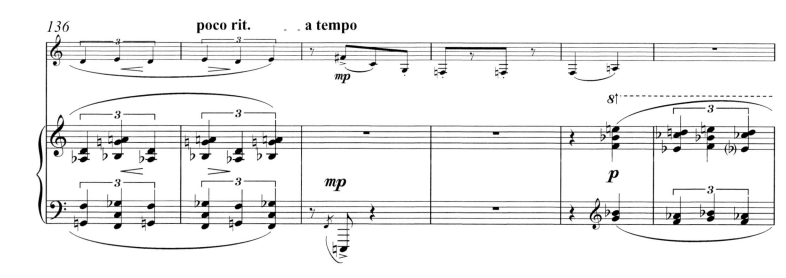

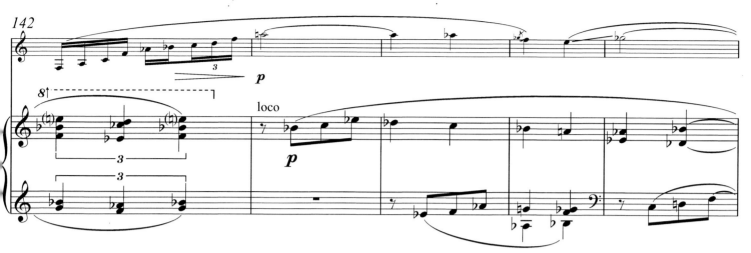

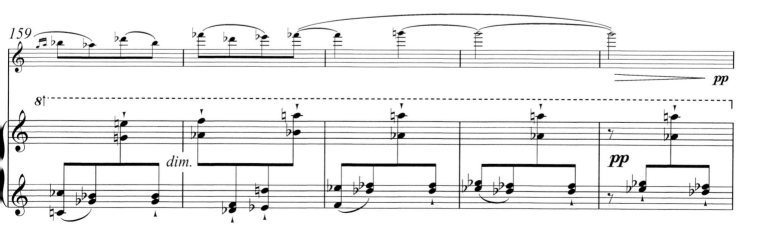

Cadenza, a piacere

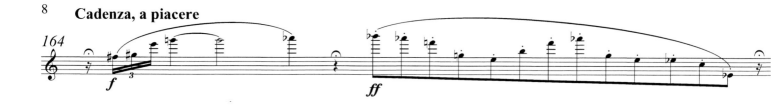

in tempo

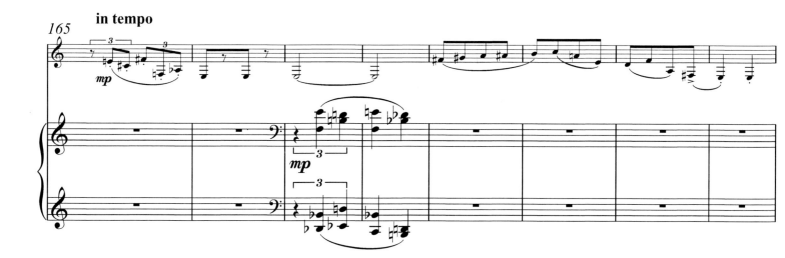

April 3, 1959

(Blank for Page Turns)

II

Presto: leggero; in 1 ♪. = 112+

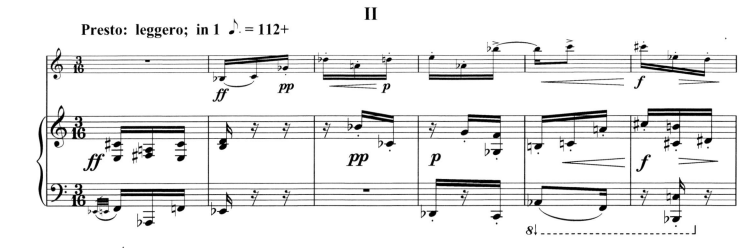

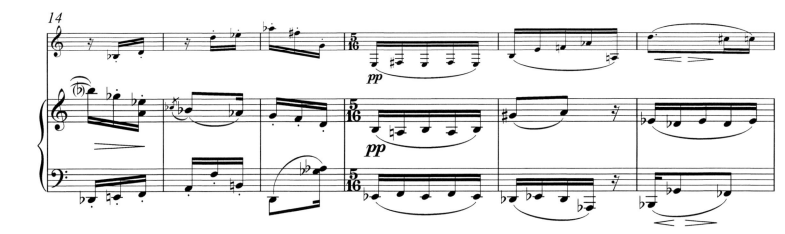

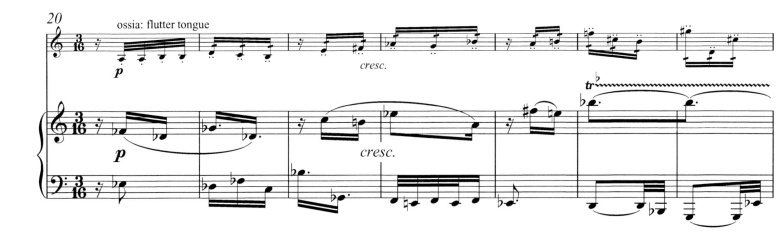

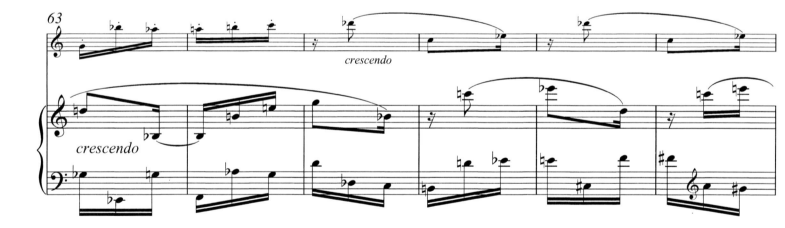

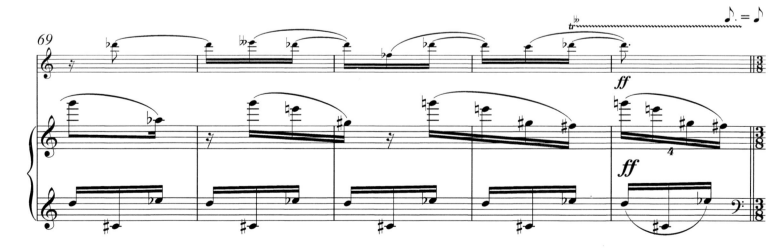

Tempo I°

ossia: flutter tongue

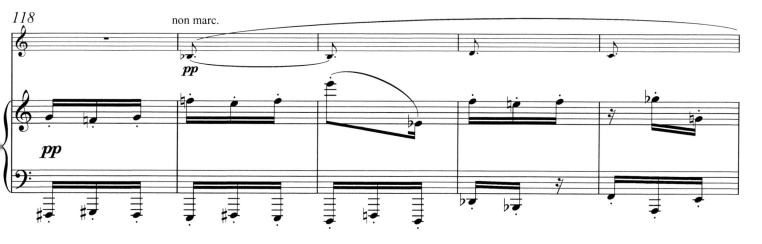

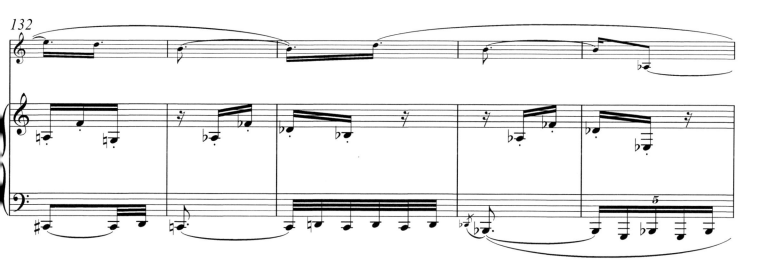

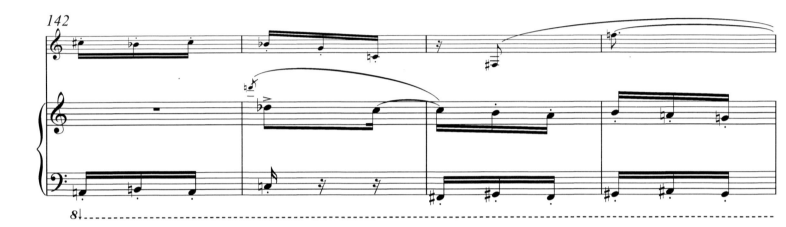

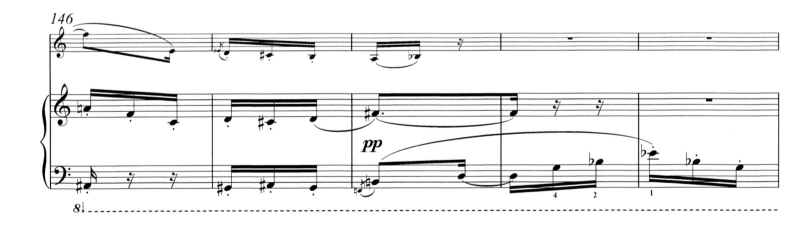

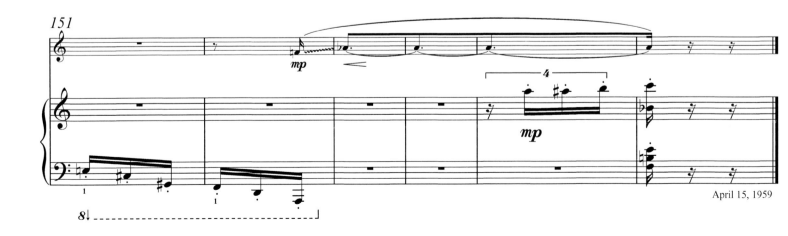

April 15, 1959

Clarinet in B♭

for Morton Subotnick

Concert-Piece
for B♭ Clarinet and Piano

I

DURATION: ca. 13:00

WILLIAM BOLCOM
(1959)

Allegro con brio ♩ = ca. 80

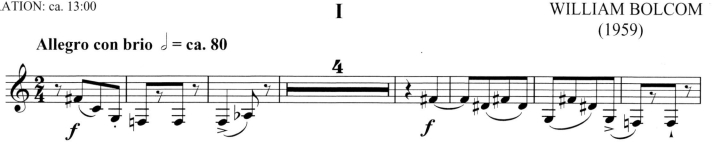

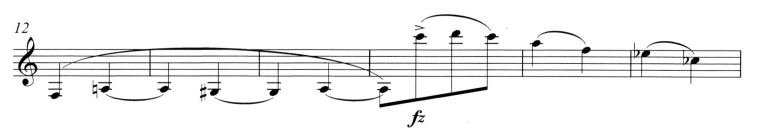

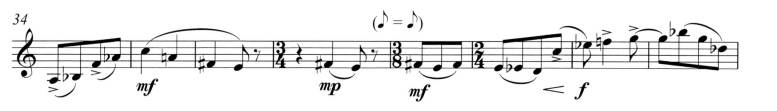

TIME

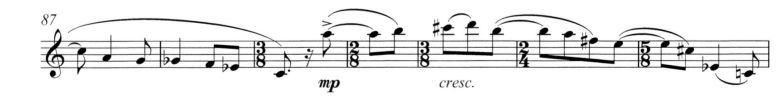

101

very short

rapide

A tempo

ff

112

2

f

119

mf

dim.

127

p

135

poco rit. _ _ **a tempo**

pp

mp

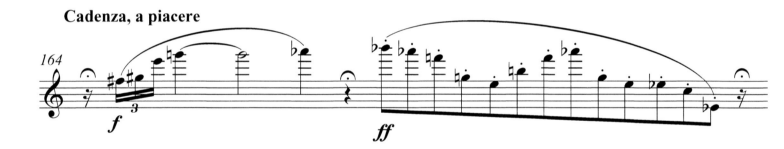

Cadenza, a piacere

in tempo

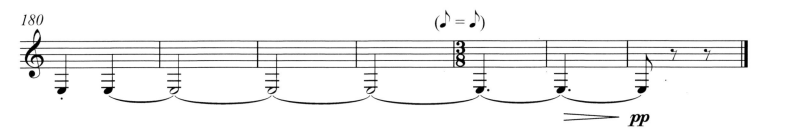

II

ossia: flutter tongue

Moderato, ma poco allegro

poch. rit. _ _ _ _ _ **poco meno mosso; _molto mesto_**

Tempo I°

ossia: flutter tongue

non marc.

TIME

III

Andante cantabile (♩ = 76-84)

Lo stesso tempo

poco allarg.   **poco meno mosso;** *ghostly*

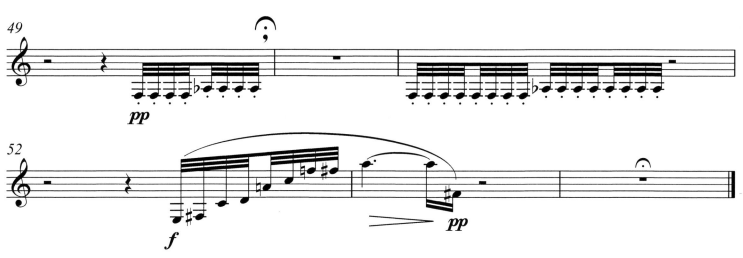

IV

Allegro giusto

growl tone

($\quad$ = $\quad$ throughout)

Clarinet in B♭

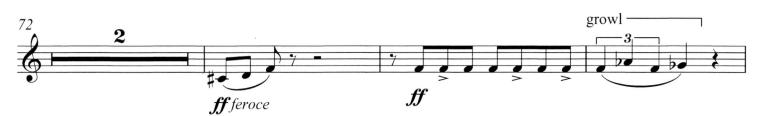

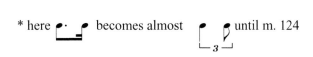

* here ♪· ♪ becomes almost ♪ ♪ until m. 124

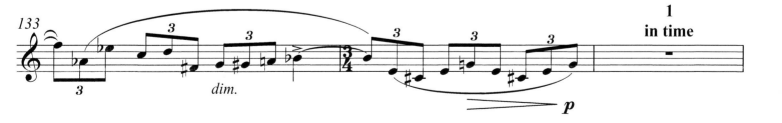

* here ♪.♪'s should be played exactly in rhythm.

III

Andante cantabile (♩ = 76-84)

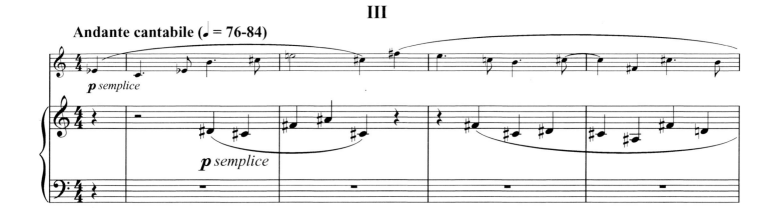

p semplice

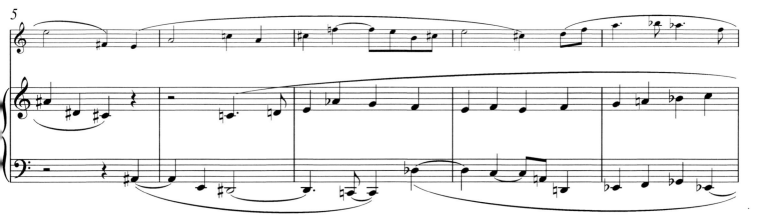

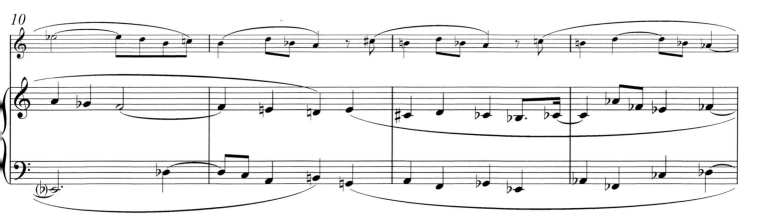

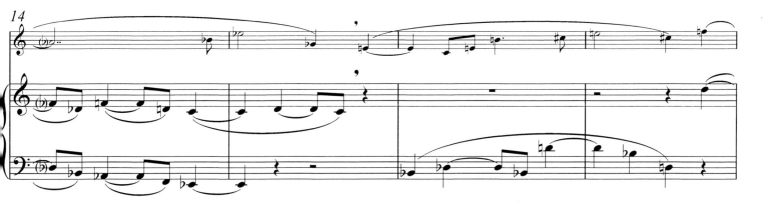

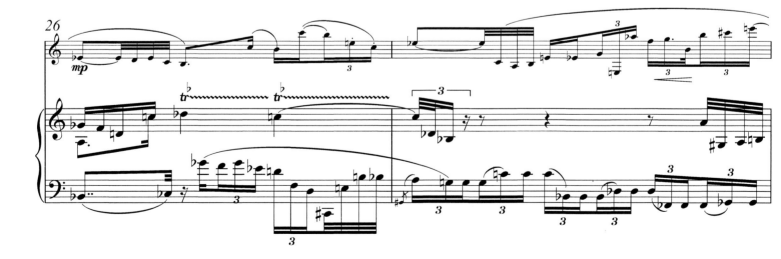

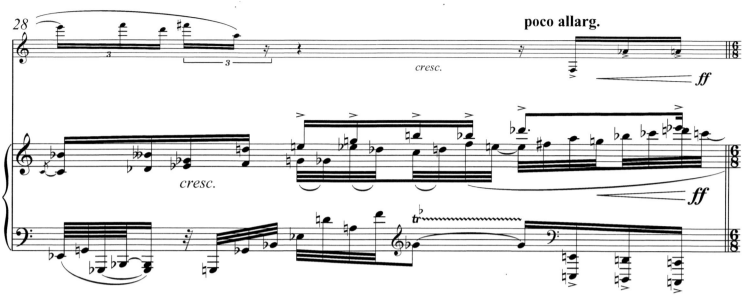

poco allarg.

poco meno mosso; *ghostly*

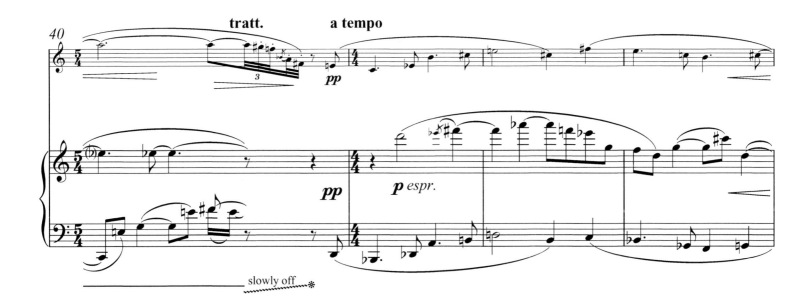

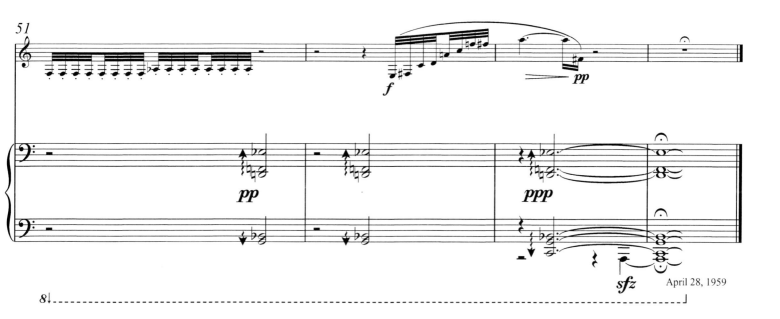

April 28, 1959

IV

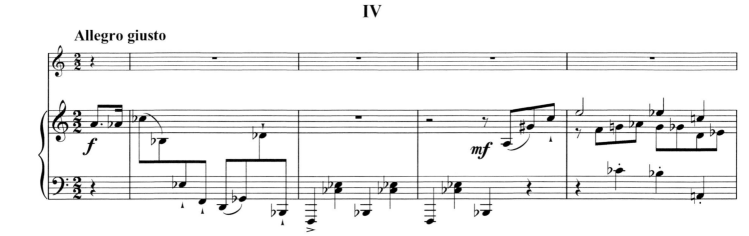

* here the rhythm should be exactly

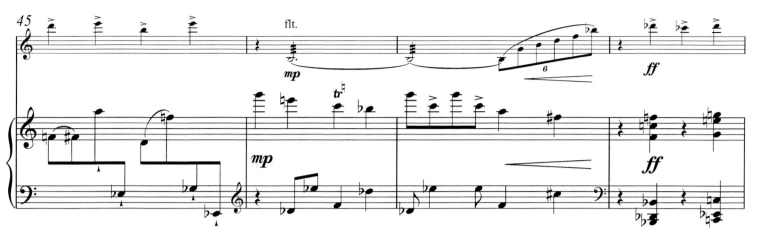

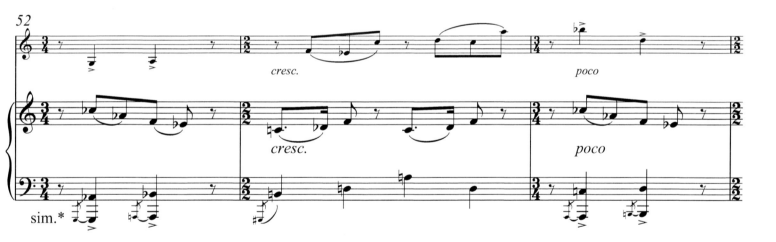

* Through m. 56, l.h. grace note should come together with r.h. notes, as in m. 51.
  In m. 56, r.h. grace note comes before the beat.

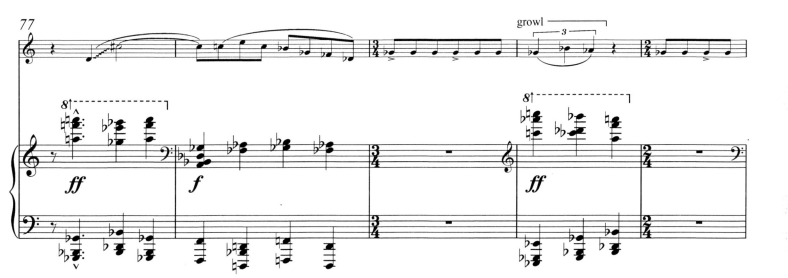

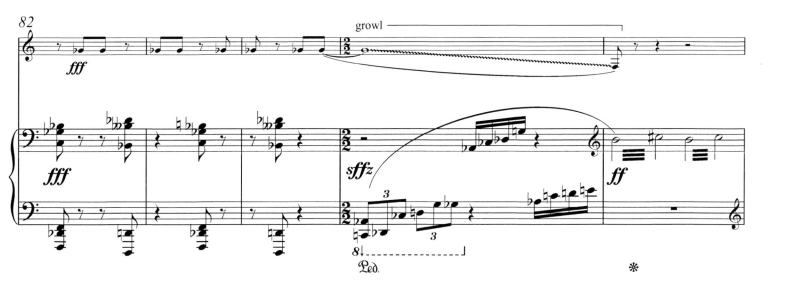

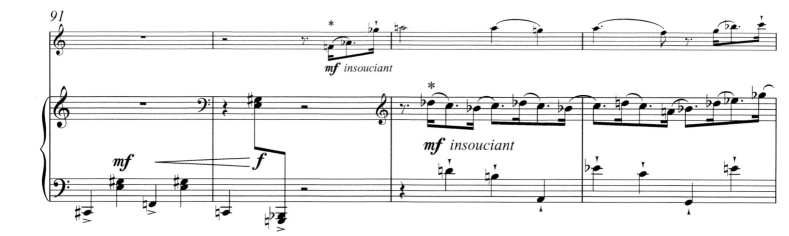

* here ♩ ♪ becomes almost ♩ ♪ until m. 124.

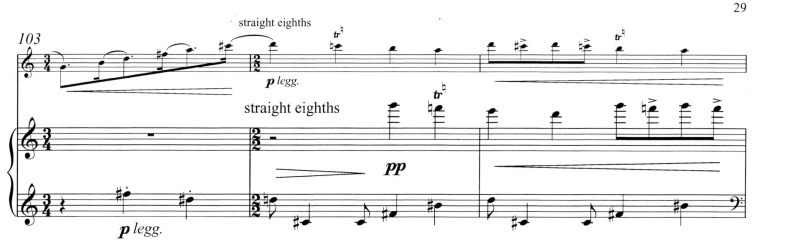

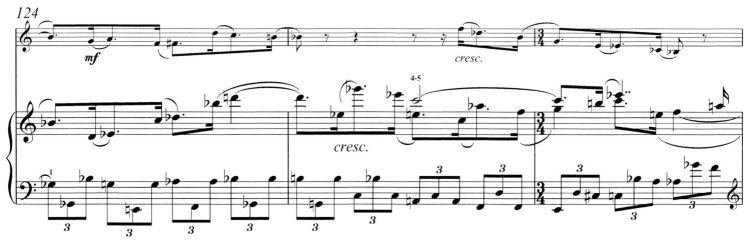

* here ♩⁀♪'s should be played exactly in rhythm.

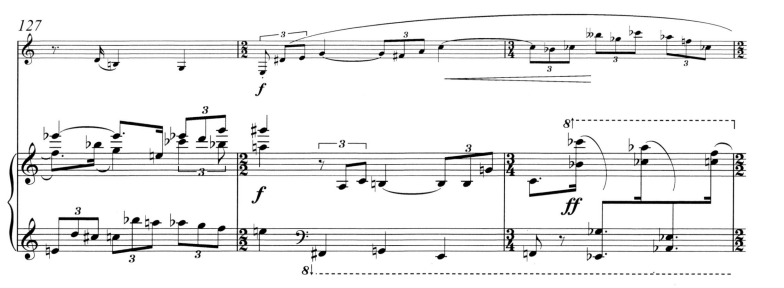

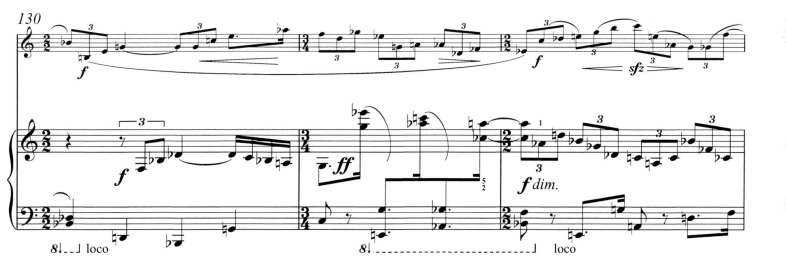

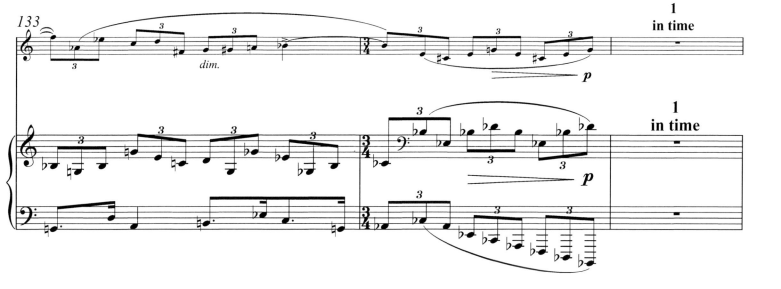

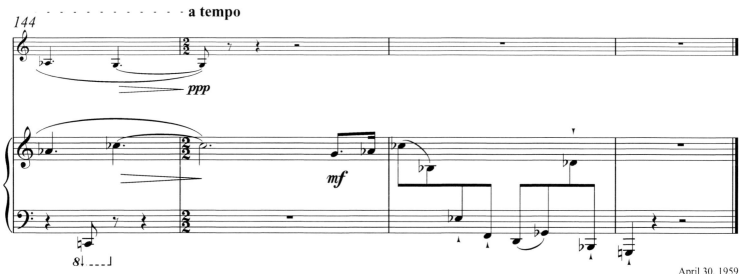

April 30, 1959
Mills College / Oakland, California